WHAT CAN HUMANS BE AS PER THE BOOK OF CREATION

David Gomadza

&

ATERY

Court of Creation Heaven

www.twofuture.world

Copyright © 2024 David Gomadza

All rights reserved.

PAPERBACK ISBN: 9798337666600

DEDICATION

New World Order

TABLE OF CONTENTS

WHAT CAN HUMANS BE AS PER THE BOOK OF CREATION 1

THE FINAL CONCLUSION 7

Predefined Parameter 1 7

Predefined Parameter 2 7

Predefined Parameter 3 7

Predefined Parameter 4 7

Predefined Parameter 5 7

Predefined Parameter 6 7

Predefined Parameter 7 8

Predefined Parameter 8 8

Predefined Parameter 9 8

Predefined Parameter 10 8

A LIST OF ALL CASES I HAVE LOOKED AT 10

1. How To Find All Missing Persons. And Collect All Reward Offers. The Formula. Volume II: THE CASE OF TONI TIKI Paperback – May 13, 2024 ... 10

2. How To Find All Missing Persons / Unsolved Cases. And Collect All Reward Offers. Volume V.: THE CASE OF DANAE WILLIAMS. Paperback – May 17, 2024 10

3. How To Find All Missing Persons And Collect All Rewards. The Formula. Volume III: THE CASE OF FAWN MARIE MOUNTAIN Paperback – May 16, 2024 10

4. How To Find All Missing Persons: And Collect All Reward Offers. THE CASE OF MADELEINE McCANN Paperback – May 9, 2024 10

5. How To Find All Missing Persons / Unsolved Cases. And Collect All Reward Offers. Volume VI: THE CASE OF CHRISTINE MARIE EASTIN Paperback – May 19, 2024 10

6. How To Find All Missing Persons / Unsolved Cases. And Collect All

Reward Offers. Volume VII.: THE CASE OF AMBER ELIZABETH CATES. Paperback – May 19, 2024 10

7. How To Find All Missing Persons. And Collect All Reward Offers. Volume IV.: THE CASE OF BRIANN MAITLAND. The Most Violent Case In History. Paperback – May 16, 2024 10

8. How To Find All Missing Persons / Unsolved Cases. And Collect All Reward Offers. Volume VIII: THE CASE OF TAMMY MAHONEY Paperback – May 21, 2024 11

9. How To Find All Missing Persons / Unsolved Cases. And Collect All Reward Offers. Volume XIII.: THE CASE OF RAELENE MAY EATON. Paperback – May 25, 2024 11

10. How To Find All Missing Persons / Unsolved Cases. And Collect All Reward Offers. Volume X.: THE CASE OF DEVON SINCLAIR MARSMAN Paperback – May 25, 2024 11

11. How To Find All Missing Persons / Unsolved Cases. And Collect All Reward Offers. Volume X1.: THE CASE OF ANNE CECILLE ZAPPELLI Paperback – May 26, 2024 11

12. How To Find All Missing Persons / Unsolved Cases. And Collect All Reward Offers. Volume XII.: THE CASE OF YVONNE KAYE WATERS Paperback – May 25, 2024 11

13. How To Find All Missing Persons / Unsolved Cases. And Collect All Reward Offers. Volume XIV.: THE CASE OF FELICIA MARIA WILSON Paperback – May 27, 2024 11

14. How To Find All Missing Persons / Unsolved Cases. And Collect All Reward Offers. Volume XV.: THE CASE OF GWENNETH GRAHAM Paperback – May 27, 2024 11

15. How To Find All Missing Persons / Unsolved Cases. And Collect All Reward Offers. Volume XVII.: THE CASE OF LAURA KATE MUCKERSIE Paperback – May 30, 2024 11

16. How To Find All Missing Persons / Unsolved Cases. And Collect All Reward Offers. Volume XX.: THE CASE OF LISA GOVAN Paperback – June 2, 2024   11

17. THE PRACTICAL GUIDE ON HOW TO SOLVE THE MISSING PERSONS OR UNSOLVED CASES WITH REWARD VALUE OF $1 Million Each.: METHODOLOGY: ALL THE TOOLS YOU NEED. Paperback – June 2, 2024...11

18. How To Find All Missing Persons / Unsolved Cases. And Collect All Reward Offers. Volume XXIV: THE CASE OF CHERYL RENWICK Paperback – June 3, 2024 11

19. How To Find All Missing Persons / Unsolved Cases. And Collect All Reward Offers. Volume XXII: THE CASE OF SHARON ELIZABETH FULTON Paperback – June 5, 2024 11

20. How To Find All Missing Persons / Unsolved Cases. And Collect All Reward Offers. Volume XXII: THE CASE OF SHARON ELIZABETH FULTON Paperback – June 5, 2024 12

21. How To Find All Missing Persons / Unsolved Cases. And Collect All Reward Offers. Volume XXV: THE CASE OF JANINE VAUGHAN Paperback – June 6, 2024 12

22. How To Find All Missing Persons / Unsolved Cases. And Collect All Reward Offers. Volume XXVI.: THE CASE OF ROBYN HICKIE Paperback – June 6, 2024 12

23. How To Find All Missing Persons / Unsolved Cases. And Collect All Reward Offers. Volume XXVII.: THE CASE OF THEO HAYEZ Paperback – June 8, 2024 12

24. How To Find All Missing Persons / Unsolved Cases. And Collect All Reward Offers. Volume XXX.: THE CASE OF JUANITA NIELSEN Paperback – June 9, 2024 12

25. How To Find All Missing Persons / Unsolved Cases. And Collect All Reward Offers. Volume XXXIII.: THE CASE OF GORDANA KOTEVSKI Paperback – June 9, 2024 12

26. How To Find All Missing Persons / Unsolved Cases. And Collect All Reward Offers. Volume XXVIII.: THE CASE OF MELISSA HUNT Paperback – June 8, 2024 12

27. How To Find All Missing Persons / Unsolved Cases. And Collect All Reward Offers. Volume XXXIV: THE CASE OF MARIA SMITH REAL NAME MARIA STERT Paperback – June 10, 2024 12

28. How To Find All Missing Persons / Unsolved Cases. And Collect All Reward Offers. Volume XXXX.: THE CASE OF PAULINE SOWRY Paperback – June 16, 2024 12

29. How To Find All Missing Persons / Unsolved Cases. And Collect All Reward Offers. Volume XXXIX.: THE CASE OF STUART SPEIES WHO SWAPPED WITH TOM PHILLIPS Paperback – June 18, 2024 12

30. How To Find All Missing Persons / Unsolved Cases. And Collect All Reward Offers. Volume XXXXI.: THE CASE OF JACK O SULLIVAN Paperback – June 18, 2024 12

31. How To Find All Missing Persons / Unsolved Cases. And Collect All Reward Offers. Volume XXXVIII.: THE CASE OF COLLEEN WALKER-GRAIG [REAL SURNAME STERT] Paperback – June 18, 2024 12

32. How To Find All Missing Persons / Unsolved Cases. And Collect All Reward Offers. Volume XXXXII.: THE CASE OF CALEB ALYN BROWN Paperback – June 19, 2024 13

33. How To Find All Missing Persons / Unsolved Cases. And Collect All Reward Offers. Volume XXXXV.: THE CASE OF JOANNE SHEEN-SMITH Paperback – June 20, 2024 13

34. The Perfect Orphans Laws And Their Rights To Their Own Property.: Extracts From The Book Of Creation Paperback – June 21, 2024 13

35. How To Find All Missing Persons / Unsolved Cases. And Collect All Reward Offers. Volume L. THE CASE OF ARLENE McLEAN Paperback – June 24, 2024 13

36. How To Find All Missing Persons / Unsolved Cases. And Collect All Reward Offers. Volume XXXXVII: THE CASE OF AS IT HAPPENS Paperback – June 24, 2024 13

37. How To Find All Missing Persons / Unsolved Cases. And Collect All Reward Offers. Volume XXXXVI.: THE CASE OF JEVELLE BALMAIN-SMITH Paperback – June 20, 2024 13

38. How To Find All Missing Persons / Unsolved Cases. And Collect All Reward Offers. Volume XXXXIX. THE CASE OF LESLIE ATN KATERNI ALSO KNOWN AS LESLIE ANNE KATNICK Paperback – June 24, 2024 13

WHAT CAN HUMANS BE AS PER THE BOOK OF CREATION

39. How To Find All Missing Persons / Unsolved Cases. And Collect All Reward Offers. Volume LII. THE CASE OF SHELTON MATHERS SANDERS Paperback – June 25, 2024 13

40. How To Find All Missing Persons / Unsolved Cases. And Collect All Reward Offers. The Formula. Volume LI. THE CASE OF SHELLEY DENISE CONNORS-THOMPSON: INCLUDES DEATH OF SEKAI SEKERUNGU Paperback – June 25, 2024 13

41. EMBEZZLED. The Missing Person Reward Scheme Is A Big Scam. In Fact A Police Reward $1million Secret $90000-Per-Account-Round Syndicate: Killing and Stealing Orphans' Houses & Creaming the Community. Paperback – June 27, 2024 13

42. THE SHELVING OF UNSOLVED CASE IS UNLAWFUL WHEN THE POLICE ARE DELIBERATELY KILLING ORPHANS AND HIDING EVIDENCE THIS WAY.: Extracted from EMBEZZLED Paperback – June 29, 2024 13

43. How To Find All Missing Persons / Unsolved Cases. And Collect All Reward Offers. The Formula. Volume LIV.: THE CASE OF ANN KIMBERLY MATHEWS McANDREW Paperback – June 29, 2024 14

44. How To Find All Missing Persons / Unsolved Cases. And Collect All Reward Offers. The Formula. Volume LV.: THE CASE OF TROY COOK Paperback – June 30, 2024 14

45. How To Find All Missing Persons / Unsolved Cases. And Collect All Reward Offers. The Formula. Volume LXII. THE CASE OF MICHAEL GERALD STEELE ROMNOP Paperback – July 4, 2024 14

46. How To Find All Missing Persons / Unsolved Cases. And Collect All Reward Offers. The Formula. Volume LVV. THE CASE OF ZACHERY LEFAVE STORN Paperback – July 4, 2024 14

47. How To Find All Missing Persons / Unsolved Cases. And Collect All Reward Offers. The Formula. Volume LXI. THE CASE OF CARSON MCNUTT Paperback – July 4, 2024 14

48. How To Find All Missing Persons / Unsolved Cases. And Collect All Reward Offers. The Formula. Volume LVIV. THE CASE OF ALLAN KENLEY MATHESON Paperback – July 4, 2024 14

49. How To Find All Missing Persons / Unsolved Cases. And Collect All

Reward Offers. The Formula. Volume LVIII. THE CASE OF IAN THOMERS MACKEGIAN Paperback – July 4, 2024 14

50. CRIMESTOPPERS' ROLE IN ABETTING AND AIDING THE POLICE IN THE KILLINGS OF ORPHANS, STEALING OF THEIR HOUSES AND IN THE SHELVING OF CASES IS UNLAWFUL. Paperback – July 4, 2024 14

51. How To Find All Missing Persons / Unsolved Cases. And Collect All Reward Offers. The Formula. Volume LIII.: THE CASE OF MARGARET ADRENALS AND MICAEL ... ASLO KNOWN AS BARRY SHERMAN AND HONEY SHERMAN Paperback – July 4, 2024 14

52. How To Find All Missing Persons / Unsolved Cases. And Collect All Reward Offers. The Formula. Volume LXIV. THE CASE OF JAESTER SLATER-JAY KNOWN AS JAY SLATER 14

53. COURT OF CREATION ON EARTH'S CASE BUNDLE THE SHELVING OF UNSOLVED CASES IS UNLAWFUL WHEN THE POLICE ARE DELIBERATELY KILLING ORPHANS AND HIDING ... NOVA SCOTIA ALL 20 MISSING PERSONS CASES. Paperback – July 8, 2024 15

54. How To Find All Missing Persons / Unsolved Cases. And Collect All Reward Offers. The Formula. Volume LVI. THE CASE OF JESS MORRISSEY-ROBERTSON JONES Paperback – July 8, 2024 15

55. COURT OF CREATION ON EARTH'S CASE BUNDLE THE SHELVING OF UNSOLVED CASES IS UNLAWFUL WHEN THE POLICE ARE DELIBERATELY KILLING ORPHANS AND HIDING ... QUEENSLAND 20 MISSING PERSONS CASES. Paperback – July 9, 2024 15

56. CREDIBLE DEFENSE TO THE ALEC BALDWIN CASE: Credible Evidence To Exonerate Alec Baldwin Paperback – July 15, 2024 15

57. COURT OF CREATION ON EARTH THE SHELVING OF UNSOLVED CASES IS UNLAWFUL WHEN THE POLICE ARE DELIBERATELY KILLING ORPHANS AND HIDING EVIDENCE THIS WAY.: UNITED STATES OF AMERICA 20 MISSING PERSONS CASES. Paperback – July 9, 2024 15

58. COURT OF CREATION ON EARTH THE SHELVING OF UNSOLVED CASES IS UNLAWFUL WHEN THE POLICE ARE DELIBERATELY KILLING ORPHANS AND HIDING EVIDENCE THIS WAY.: BRITAIN 20 MISSING PERSONS CASES. Paperback – July 9, 2024 15

59. How To Find All Missing Persons / Unsolved Cases. And Collect All Reward Offers. Volume LIX. THE CASE OF THE VICTIMS OF POLICE OFFICER ASEROPERS CATERINA Paperback – July 22, 2024 15

60. How To Find All Missing Persons / Unsolved Cases. And Collect All Reward Offers. Volume LVIII. THE CASE OF MATTHEW PERRY AND EL INE PARK-TSU Paperback – July 22, 2024 15

61. How To Live Up To 1 Million Years Looking Like When You Were 2 Years Old: hailhailhailodavidgomadza.startx8.initialise.start Paperback – July 24, 2024 15

62. Introducing Nickel As The New Currency Paperback – July 25, 2024 16

63. COURT OF CREATION ON EARTH THE SHELVING OF UNSOLVED CASES IS UNLAWFUL WHEN THE POLICE ARE DELIBERATELY KILLING ORPHANS AND HIDING EVIDENCE THIS WAY.: NEW ZEALAND Paperback – July 9, 2024 16

64. How To Find All Missing Persons / Unsolved Cases And Collect All Reward Offers The Formula. Volume LXX THE CASE OF THE VICTIMS OF POLICE OFFICER AEROSITY AEROSTY Paperback – July 31, 2024 16

65. How to Find All Missing Persons / Unsolved Cases and Collect All Reward Offers. The Formula. Volume LXXI THE CASE OF ELLE ESTELLE-PARKINSON Paperback – August 3, 2024 16

66. How To Find All Missing Persons / Unsolved Cases And Collect All Reward Offers The Formula. Volume LXXII. NEW ZEALAND. THE CASE OF THE VICTIMS OF POLICE OFFICER ASEROSTY ASEROSITY Paperback – August 6, 2024 16

67. How To Find All Missing Persons / Unsolved Cases And Collect All Reward Offers The Formula. Volume LXXIII. NEW ZEALAND & AUSTRALIA THE CASE OF THE VICTIMS OF POLICE OFFICER ATERSER AOTAOA Paperback – August 8, 2024 16

68. How To Find All Missing Persons / Unsolved Cases And Collect All Reward Offers The Formula. Volume LXXIV. BRITAIN, GERMANY, DUTCH BRAZIL & NEW ... VICTIMS OF POLICE OFFICER ATENOSTY ATENOSITY Paperback – August 9, 2024 16

69.   How to Find All Missing Persons / Unsolved Cases and Collect All Reward Offers the Formula. Volume LXXV. BRITAIN. THE CASE OF THE VICTIMS OF POLICE OFFICER ATENOSTY ATENOSTY: [continued] Paperback – August 10, 2024...16

70.   Earth2 What Can Be of Humans with And Without YAHWEH's Creation and How to Resolve the Issues Raised. A Look at Creation and YAHWEH's Adjustments' Implications on Humans 21 August 2024...........17

ACKNOWLEDGMENTS

Tomorrow's World Order

WHAT CAN HUMANS BE AS PER THE BOOK OF CREATION

Predefined parameters are parameters set by the creator to guide his creation into something he wants and want to work the way he want it to work in other words they are working parameters that guide everything if a human from breathing to death and even after death these make sure that the human being live a normal healthy lifestyle full of energy and activities because the purpose is To tell the body what it can do and must do throughout life so that the experience gained manifest itself in boxes of predefined parameters where everything achieved is documented and to be presented at birth to redirect the person to the correct afterlife if you were not interested in seeing heaven might not be for you and another place can be chosen for you so all what is the fact that humans must achieve everything as predefined parameters to be assigned the correct place when death comes knocking now let's look at all predefined parameters here is a list the first is to do with Creation These are to do with life and death and how the body must react in terms of these and must be abided by for a human being to enjoy full life and must abide by these failures will result in some of the predefined parameters removed at the end when death come knocking now what are precreation predefined parameters? These regulate the life that is being created and must be in consistence with creation meaning if a human being chooses to ignore any of the commands then the predefined are to be useless

WHAT CAN HUMANS BE AS PER THE BOOK OF CREATION

hence in the end they might be removed as unused hence unwanted or pointless but if needed they can still be incorporated into the next design hence these must take over and control the creation now let's look at some examples where a human being has precreation predefined hence we must know what these are

1. Do not live and die then live aim to live live live then die this means that its unlogic for any human being to think of living then dying then reliving again this means that humans must aim to make the most of the time they have as humans then ask to be relieved of living hoping to come back at some time in the future if we ask what can be of humans that think too much then this is the answer they waste time procrastinating rather than getting on with life

2. If we are to ask what can be of humans that waste time thinking and not acting then this is the answer they miss opportunities to create wealth because time does not wait for any men but some men can make time wait for them but this is rare a once in a lifetime opportunity and this is the only time this has happened and probably will never happen again [David Gomadza] so if we ask what can be of humans that an work fast and make wealth these are the ones that can make things happen as time is on their side they have wealth and everything hence all they need is a bit of lucky for the wheel of fortune to be at the right place for them to make a fortune if we look at what can be of these people here is the list of things they can easily accomplish

   a] they can make appointment with the creators of other things and invest in their research etc.

   b] they can calculate when to invest in other people's investments and make it big when they reap benefits

   c] they can always be prepared for anything to invest and make big rewards as this is the only way in life to make money the rest is just talking bullshit

   d] if we ask what can be of people with no money but time then they keep procrastinating about money because now they found time but time alone can't make money you need a great business plan to start but the only thing is that they are in great shape to start anything and the sky is the only

WHAT CAN HUMANS BE AS PER THE BOOK OF CREATION

limit

e] if we can ask what can be of people like him then this is the answer it might take even more time to strike it big but when they make it them beat everyone else because their plans can't be matched by anyone but if we look at those who are successful most become successful then die leaving all the wealth in the hand s of family members this has been the trend with all humans but we might see a new way of doing things with David Gomadza as he has embarked on looking for longevity then search for the fortune and if this works he will have solved THE GREAT INTELLIGENCE RIDDLE by Waaaaaer Yahweh $00000^{38}9$ where he talked about how he can postpone everything and look for a way to increase longevity as in the book of creation telling people that everyone who finds longevity first is the greatest human being to live on earth which he did but only after death and now we have his own follower achieving his dream and this is remarkable because what are the odds of something like this happening surely he is the best creator ever if he can guide his own created being to fulfill his dreams while his follower

Now let's look at other predefined parameters

Birth predefined 2800
Life predefined 1700
Death 700
Eternity 600
After eternity 200
After after eternity 160
Afterlife 100

The body must obey all predefined parameters to exist forever any breach of the predefined will result in death at any stage if you walk when the body wants you to sit can result in death as well but this does not include endurance as endurance is automatically excluded as some people push themselves to the limit all predefined parameters cannot be adjusted after birth as the body seals these forever so that no adjustments can be made but you can alter some height is a predefined parameters there is no person

WHAT CAN HUMANS BE AS PER THE BOOK OF CREATION

who grew taller after reaching limit but weight is not a predefined the reason is that everything else must change if height changes which is impossible

Things to do for humans as in the book of creation
Ask.davidgomadza.bookofcreation.thingstodoforhumans.start
The book of creation requires people in humans to obey certain rules so that humans remain humans but there are others that are needed so that humans excel and do well I will list 110 things humans must do to excel as required by Yahweh

1. Arise to the top early with what power agility reason charm
2. Ask what can be done early? Who .ya
3. Ask what could be of human's creator predators
4. Ask what is to be of humans any creature [creator]
5. Ask what can be of humans anything [creator]
6. Ask what is of humans prohibit to be others can't be [angels]
7. Ask what was of human's aliens until Yahweh created earth
8. Ask what could be of humans anything [creator]
9. Ask what is of humans anything [creator]
10. Ask what was of human's death [only 1 achieved longevity]
11. Ask what can be of humans anything [creator]
12. Ask if not us then who angels [wings need unsealing]
13. If us then when anytime [now]
14. If us then with what power agility reason charm vindication
15. If us then with whom angels' god's creator
16. If not them then with who alone
17. What is to be of humans can be anything
18. What can be of human's great creators intelligent
19. What is to be of human's humans can be anything
20. What was humans alien shadow no foresight?
21. What could be humans' creators
22. What was but can still be death ignorance
23. What could be but can't be human greatness
24. If not these then who angels
25. What would be human anything angels' creators
26. What was humans alien but not any more
27. What can be human gods live longer be wise
28. What is to be human creators in the end

WHAT CAN HUMANS BE AS PER THE BOOK OF CREATION

29. What can be human anything [angels gods creator]
30. What is to be human death but
31. What was human death
32. What could be human anything] if not these then who with what angels' knowledge
33. What I but can't be human angels
34. What would be human creator
35. What would human be magnificent creator
36. What can be human creator
37. What human is not death not creator but can be taught to be
38. What can be human anything creator
39. What human can be power agility charm vindication
40. What is but can't be ignorance
41. What human is earthly creator
42. What is human but is not human creator
43. What was human but can still be human death ignorance what was but is not steadiness
44. What can be but is not god [don't move]
45. What would be but is not nothing what can be but might not be creator status
46. If we are then with who gods without too much controlling
47. If not then why too challenging if not but why and too challenging without for short time
48. If not us then who god's creator
49. What is to be but can't be nothing
50. what was but is not ignorance obstacles removed
51. if not human then who gods and creator
52. if human but with what knowledge agility power
53. why not us if human is not then why and where nothing if not human then who god's creator but human
54. what can be human but is not gods
55. what is human creator
56. what can be human creator
57. What was human lack of foresight
58. What human can be creator
59. What humans can't be nothing
60. What is to be human power charm agility vindication

WHAT CAN HUMANS BE AS PER THE BOOK OF CREATION

61. If not human then what creator
62. If not human then what creator
63. If not human then who creator
64. If not us then who and when creator anytime
65. What can be human but is not human creator
66. What human can be creator
67. What is to be human creator
68. What could be human creator
69. If not human then what creator
70. What can be human creator
71. What if human creator
72. What can be human creator
73. If not human then what creator
74. What is human creator
75. What can be human creator
76. What is to be human creator
77. What human is creator
78. What is to be human creator
79. What could human be creator
80. What human is knowledge power charm agility
81. If not human then what is creator
82. What can be but is not human creator
83. Humans can be what else knowledgeable
84. What else can be humans' creators
85. If not now then when now
86. If not now then with what knowledge
87. If not human then what creator
88. If human then with what knowledge
89. What can be but is not creator
90. If not all humans then who else creator
91. What if knowledge power agility charm
92. What was ignorance death
93. What can be ignorance death
94. What could be ignorance death
95. What was but is not ignorance
96. If not humans then who creator
97. Humans with what knowledge power agility charm vindication

WHAT CAN HUMANS BE AS PER THE BOOK OF CREATION

98. Humans with who creator
99. Humans and what knowledge power agility vindication charm
100. Humans who are human's creator
101. Humans can be gods no
102. Humans can be creator yes
103. First human creator David Gomadza in terms of long ago at $8989898989^{789838682848902867898238}$ sec longest ever

THE FINAL CONCLUSION

Other Predefined Parameters.

Predefined Parameter 1

What is life the right to breath freely

Predefined Parameter 2

What could be of life with ya and without ya so you are shown life without ya and with ya and choose

Predefined Parameter 3

What is ya it's a network of God and creator as a human and Yahweh and creator for angels

Predefined Parameter 4

What is life with .ya it's a life of submission and honor you cannot say Yahweh or God in danger otherwise you will lose your life

Predefined Parameter 5

You cannot ask other creatures for help but you can ask for advice

Predefined Parameter 6

What could be of the book f creation the book of creation includes all chapters on humans that need to be covered by humans like how can we achieve greatness and what is human humans are the 7th creatures of earth after the other 6 planets

1. zoles
2. oer
3. ost

4. ovm
5. opm
6. otu

now if we ask what can be of all these then all these are the most advanced of all in hierarchy with each worth billion in US$ value but with little ways of translating this into real value until now we have news a nickel currency is in testing mode that can mean a better future for all of us send message create.sendallnickeldepositstoreservebankofunitedstateofamericaunderthenamedavidgomadza.start

if we ask what can be of human with nickel the best as a medium of exchange but was removed because it became hard to find nickel after the second world war as some was burnt to make bullets but now could be enough to justify starting again humans can be told what to do without objections and can say what can be of them without issues humans can be anything they want to be what was humans can still be meaning even after another 18 billion years humans can still be humans the book of creation is the basis of all creatures all creatures have a chapter on the book of creation

Predefined Parameter 7

The book of creation teaches us how to ask for help when needed

Predefined Parameter 8

It is the way humans must live they must ask what can be and what could be of humans now and in the future and know in advance what is Yahweh's curse you kill me you die in 8 days as per the book of creation

Predefined Parameter 9

Ask ya all the time but for beginners only and for the experienced never ask for Yahweh or he will take your life for stressing him once a year for his representative just to update him on progress and never for humans or risk death

Predefined Parameter 10

I am the guiding force in life people who access this file in early ages always became successful do you no human has ever opened predefined parameter 10 you are the first I ask 22 questions that will guide me to you these are

WHAT CAN HUMANS BE AS PER THE BOOK OF CREATION

1. What can you do in life
2. What is to be of the creator and humans in your eyes
3. What could be of humans in the creator eyes
4. What was and what is of the creator
5. How can we improve relationships?
6. How can we find solutions to our problems?
7. how can we find solutions on a large scale?
8. what is that what humans must do
9. what can be of humans without ya
10. what is ya
11. how ya is different from Zeus
12. humans must not be told how to fill the boxes but if they find out themselves then its only through hard work
13. what was and might still be of you
14. what has been of you
15. what could be of you
16. what must be of you
17. what can be of you
18. what is to be of you
19. what was and could still be you
20. what can be of you and them
21. what was and still be of them
22. what will be of them

FURTHER READING

A LIST OF ALL CASES I HAVE LOOKED AT

1. How To Find All Missing Persons. And Collect All Reward Offers. The Formula. Volume II: THE CASE OF TONI TIKI Paperback – May 13, 2024
2. How To Find All Missing Persons / Unsolved Cases. And Collect All Reward Offers. Volume V.: THE CASE OF DANAE WILLIAMS. Paperback – May 17, 2024
3. How To Find All Missing Persons And Collect All Rewards. The Formula. Volume III: THE CASE OF FAWN MARIE MOUNTAIN Paperback – May 16, 2024
4. How To Find All Missing Persons: And Collect All Reward Offers. THE CASE OF MADELEINE McCANN Paperback – May 9, 2024
5. How To Find All Missing Persons / Unsolved Cases. And Collect All Reward Offers. Volume VI: THE CASE OF CHRISTINE MARIE EASTIN Paperback – May 19, 2024
6. How To Find All Missing Persons / Unsolved Cases. And Collect All Reward Offers. Volume VII.: THE CASE OF AMBER ELIZABETH CATES. Paperback – May 19, 2024
7. How To Find All Missing Persons. And Collect All Reward Offers. Volume IV.: THE CASE OF BRIANN MAITLAND. The Most Violent Case In History. Paperback – May 16, 2024

8. How To Find All Missing Persons / Unsolved Cases. And Collect All Reward Offers. Volume VIII: THE CASE OF TAMMY MAHONEY Paperback – May 21, 2024
9. How To Find All Missing Persons / Unsolved Cases. And Collect All Reward Offers. Volume XIII.: THE CASE OF RAELENE MAY EATON. Paperback – May 25, 2024
10. How To Find All Missing Persons / Unsolved Cases. And Collect All Reward Offers. Volume X.: THE CASE OF DEVON SINCLAIR MARSMAN Paperback – May 25, 2024
11. How To Find All Missing Persons / Unsolved Cases. And Collect All Reward Offers. Volume X1.: THE CASE OF ANNE CECILLE ZAPPELLI Paperback – May 26, 2024
12. How To Find All Missing Persons / Unsolved Cases. And Collect All Reward Offers. Volume XII.: THE CASE OF YVONNE KAYE WATERS Paperback – May 25, 2024
13. How To Find All Missing Persons / Unsolved Cases. And Collect All Reward Offers. Volume XIV.: THE CASE OF FELICIA MARIA WILSON Paperback – May 27, 2024
14. How To Find All Missing Persons / Unsolved Cases. And Collect All Reward Offers. Volume XV.: THE CASE OF GWENNETH GRAHAM Paperback – May 27, 2024
15. How To Find All Missing Persons / Unsolved Cases. And Collect All Reward Offers. Volume XVII.: THE CASE OF LAURA KATE MUCKERSIE Paperback – May 30, 2024
16. How To Find All Missing Persons / Unsolved Cases. And Collect All Reward Offers. Volume XX.: THE CASE OF LISA GOVAN Paperback – June 2, 2024
17. THE PRACTICAL GUIDE ON HOW TO SOLVE THE MISSING PERSONS OR UNSOLVED CASES WITH REWARD VALUE OF $1 Million Each.: METHODOLOGY: ALL THE TOOLS YOU NEED. Paperback – June 2, 2024
18. How To Find All Missing Persons / Unsolved Cases. And Collect All Reward Offers. Volume XXIV: THE CASE OF CHERYL RENWICK Paperback – June 3, 2024
19. How To Find All Missing Persons / Unsolved Cases. And Collect All Reward Offers. Volume XXII: THE CASE OF SHARON ELIZABETH FULTON Paperback – June 5, 2024

20. How To Find All Missing Persons / Unsolved Cases. And Collect All Reward Offers. Volume XXII: THE CASE OF SHARON ELIZABETH FULTON Paperback – June 5, 2024
21. How To Find All Missing Persons / Unsolved Cases. And Collect All Reward Offers. Volume XXV: THE CASE OF JANINE VAUGHAN Paperback – June 6, 2024
22. How To Find All Missing Persons / Unsolved Cases. And Collect All Reward Offers. Volume XXVI.: THE CASE OF ROBYN HICKIE Paperback – June 6, 2024
23. How To Find All Missing Persons / Unsolved Cases. And Collect All Reward Offers. Volume XXVII.: THE CASE OF THEO HAYEZ Paperback – June 8, 2024
24. How To Find All Missing Persons / Unsolved Cases. And Collect All Reward Offers. Volume XXX.: THE CASE OF JUANITA NIELSEN Paperback – June 9, 2024
25. How To Find All Missing Persons / Unsolved Cases. And Collect All Reward Offers. Volume XXXIII.: THE CASE OF GORDANA KOTEVSKI Paperback – June 9, 2024
26. How To Find All Missing Persons / Unsolved Cases. And Collect All Reward Offers. Volume XXVIII.: THE CASE OF MELISSA HUNT Paperback – June 8, 2024
27. How To Find All Missing Persons / Unsolved Cases. And Collect All Reward Offers. Volume XXXIV: THE CASE OF MARIA SMITH REAL NAME MARIA STERT Paperback – June 10, 2024
28. How To Find All Missing Persons / Unsolved Cases. And Collect All Reward Offers. Volume XXXX.: THE CASE OF PAULINE SOWRY Paperback – June 16, 2024
29. How To Find All Missing Persons / Unsolved Cases. And Collect All Reward Offers. Volume XXXIX.: THE CASE OF STUART SPEIES WHO SWAPPED WITH TOM PHILLIPS Paperback – June 18, 2024
30. How To Find All Missing Persons / Unsolved Cases. And Collect All Reward Offers. Volume XXXXI.: THE CASE OF JACK O SULLIVAN Paperback – June 18, 2024
31. How To Find All Missing Persons / Unsolved Cases. And Collect All Reward Offers. Volume XXXVIII.: THE CASE OF

COLLEEN WALKER-GRAIG [REAL SURNAME STERT] Paperback – June 18, 2024

32. How To Find All Missing Persons / Unsolved Cases. And Collect All Reward Offers. Volume XXXXII.: THE CASE OF CALEB ALYN BROWN Paperback – June 19, 2024

33. How To Find All Missing Persons / Unsolved Cases. And Collect All Reward Offers. Volume XXXXV.: THE CASE OF JOANNE SHEEN-SMITH Paperback – June 20, 2024

34. The Perfect Orphans Laws And Their Rights To Their Own Property.: Extracts From The Book Of Creation Paperback – June 21, 2024

35. How To Find All Missing Persons / Unsolved Cases. And Collect All Reward Offers. Volume L. THE CASE OF ARLENE McLEAN Paperback – June 24, 2024

36. How To Find All Missing Persons / Unsolved Cases. And Collect All Reward Offers. Volume XXXXVII: THE CASE OF AS IT HAPPENS Paperback – June 24, 2024

37. How To Find All Missing Persons / Unsolved Cases. And Collect All Reward Offers. Volume XXXXVI.: THE CASE OF JEVELLE BALMAIN-SMITH Paperback – June 20, 2024

38. How To Find All Missing Persons / Unsolved Cases. And Collect All Reward Offers. Volume XXXXIX. THE CASE OF LESLIE ATN KATERNI ALSO KNOWN AS LESLIE ANNE KATNICK Paperback – June 24, 2024

39. How To Find All Missing Persons / Unsolved Cases. And Collect All Reward Offers. Volume LII. THE CASE OF SHELTON MATHERS SANDERS Paperback – June 25, 2024

40. How To Find All Missing Persons / Unsolved Cases. And Collect All Reward Offers. The Formula. Volume LI. THE CASE OF SHELLEY DENISE CONNORS-THOMPSON: INCLUDES DEATH OF SEKAI SEKERUNGU Paperback – June 25, 2024

41. EMBEZZLED. The Missing Person Reward Scheme Is A Big Scam. In Fact A Police Reward $1million Secret $90000-Per-Account-Round Syndicate: Killing and Stealing Orphans' Houses & Creaming the Community. Paperback – June 27, 2024

42. THE SHELVING OF UNSOLVED CASE IS UNLAWFUL WHEN THE POLICE ARE DELIBERATELY KILLING ORPHANS AND HIDING

WHAT CAN HUMANS BE AS PER THE BOOK OF CREATION

EVIDENCE THIS WAY.: Extracted from EMBEZZLED Paperback – June 29, 2024

43. How To Find All Missing Persons / Unsolved Cases. And Collect All Reward Offers. The Formula. Volume LIV.: THE CASE OF ANN KIMBERLY MATHEWS McANDREW Paperback – June 29, 2024
44. How To Find All Missing Persons / Unsolved Cases. And Collect All Reward Offers. The Formula. Volume LV.: THE CASE OF TROY COOK Paperback – June 30, 2024
45. How To Find All Missing Persons / Unsolved Cases. And Collect All Reward Offers. The Formula. Volume LXII. THE CASE OF MICHAEL GERALD STEELE ROMNOP Paperback – July 4, 2024
46. How To Find All Missing Persons / Unsolved Cases. And Collect All Reward Offers. The Formula. Volume LVV. THE CASE OF ZACHERY LEFAVE STORN Paperback – July 4, 2024
47. How To Find All Missing Persons / Unsolved Cases. And Collect All Reward Offers. The Formula. Volume LXI. THE CASE OF CARSON MCNUTT Paperback – July 4, 2024
48. How To Find All Missing Persons / Unsolved Cases. And Collect All Reward Offers. The Formula. Volume LVIV. THE CASE OF ALLAN KENLEY MATHESON Paperback – July 4, 2024
49. How To Find All Missing Persons / Unsolved Cases. And Collect All Reward Offers. The Formula. Volume LVIII. THE CASE OF IAN THOMERS MACKEGIAN Paperback – July 4, 2024
50. CRIMESTOPPERS' ROLE IN ABETTING AND AIDING THE POLICE IN THE KILLINGS OF ORPHANS, STEALING OF THEIR HOUSES AND IN THE SHELVING OF CASES IS UNLAWFUL. Paperback – July 4, 2024
51. How To Find All Missing Persons / Unsolved Cases. And Collect All Reward Offers. The Formula. Volume LIII.: THE CASE OF MARGARET ADRENALS AND MICAEL ... ASLO KNOWN AS BARRY SHERMAN AND HONEY SHERMAN Paperback – July 4, 2024
52. How To Find All Missing Persons / Unsolved Cases. And Collect All Reward Offers. The Formula. Volume LXIV. THE CASE OF JAESTER SLATER-JAY KNOWN AS JAY SLATER

53. COURT OF CREATION ON EARTH'S CASE BUNDLE THE SHELVING OF UNSOLVED CASES IS UNLAWFUL WHEN THE POLICE ARE DELIBERATELY KILLING ORPHANS AND HIDING ... NOVA SCOTIA ALL 20 MISSING PERSONS CASES. Paperback – July 8, 2024
54. How To Find All Missing Persons / Unsolved Cases. And Collect All Reward Offers. The Formula. Volume LVI. THE CASE OF JESS MORRISSEY-ROBERTSON JONES Paperback – July 8, 2024
55. COURT OF CREATION ON EARTH'S CASE BUNDLE THE SHELVING OF UNSOLVED CASES IS UNLAWFUL WHEN THE POLICE ARE DELIBERATELY KILLING ORPHANS AND HIDING ... QUEENSLAND 20 MISSING PERSONS CASES. Paperback – July 9, 2024
56. CREDIBLE DEFENSE TO THE ALEC BALDWIN CASE: Credible Evidence To Exonerate Alec Baldwin Paperback – July 15, 2024
57. COURT OF CREATION ON EARTH THE SHELVING OF UNSOLVED CASES IS UNLAWFUL WHEN THE POLICE ARE DELIBERATELY KILLING ORPHANS AND HIDING EVIDENCE THIS WAY.: UNITED STATES OF AMERICA 20 MISSING PERSONS CASES. Paperback – July 9, 2024
58. COURT OF CREATION ON EARTH THE SHELVING OF UNSOLVED CASES IS UNLAWFUL WHEN THE POLICE ARE DELIBERATELY KILLING ORPHANS AND HIDING EVIDENCE THIS WAY.: BRITAIN 20 MISSING PERSONS CASES. Paperback – July 9, 2024
59. How To Find All Missing Persons / Unsolved Cases. And Collect All Reward Offers. Volume LIX. THE CASE OF THE VICTIMS OF POLICE OFFICER ASEROPERS CATERINA Paperback – July 22, 2024
60. How To Find All Missing Persons / Unsolved Cases. And Collect All Reward Offers. Volume LVIII. THE CASE OF MATTHEW PERRY AND EL INE PARK-TSU Paperback – July 22, 2024
61. How To Live Up To 1 Million Years Looking Like When You Were 2 Years Old:

WHAT CAN HUMANS BE AS PER THE BOOK OF CREATION

hailhailhailodavidgomadza.startx8.initialise.start Paperback – July 24, 2024

62. Introducing Nickel As The New Currency Paperback – July 25, 2024
63. COURT OF CREATION ON EARTH THE SHELVING OF UNSOLVED CASES IS UNLAWFUL WHEN THE POLICE ARE DELIBERATELY KILLING ORPHANS AND HIDING EVIDENCE THIS WAY.: NEW ZEALAND Paperback – July 9, 2024
64. How To Find All Missing Persons / Unsolved Cases And Collect All Reward Offers The Formula. Volume LXX THE CASE OF THE VICTIMS OF POLICE OFFICER AEROSITY AEROSTY Paperback – July 31, 2024
65. How to Find All Missing Persons / Unsolved Cases and Collect All Reward Offers. The Formula. Volume LXXI THE CASE OF ELLE ESTELLE-PARKINSON Paperback – August 3, 2024
66. How To Find All Missing Persons / Unsolved Cases And Collect All Reward Offers The Formula. Volume LXXII. NEW ZEALAND. THE CASE OF THE VICTIMS OF POLICE OFFICER ASEROSTY ASEROSITY Paperback – August 6, 2024
67. How To Find All Missing Persons / Unsolved Cases And Collect All Reward Offers The Formula. Volume LXXIII. NEW ZEALAND & AUSTRALIA THE CASE OF THE VICTIMS OF POLICE OFFICER ATERSER AOTAOA Paperback – August 8, 2024
68. How To Find All Missing Persons / Unsolved Cases And Collect All Reward Offers The Formula. Volume LXXIV. BRITAIN, GERMANY, DUTCH BRAZIL & NEW … VICTIMS OF POLICE OFFICER ATENOSTY ATENOSITY Paperback – August 9, 2024
69. How to Find All Missing Persons / Unsolved Cases and Collect All Reward Offers the Formula. Volume LXXV. BRITAIN. THE CASE OF THE VICTIMS OF POLICE OFFICER ATENOSTY ATENOSITY: [continued] Paperback – August 10, 2024

WHAT CAN HUMANS BE AS PER THE BOOK OF CREATION

70. Earth2 What Can Be of Humans with And Without YAHWEH's Creation and How to Resolve the Issues Raised. A Look at Creation and YAHWEH's Adjustments' Implications on Humans 21 August 2024
71. B] THE SHELVING OF UNSOLVED CASE IS UNLAWFUL WHEN THE POLICE ARE DELIBERATELY KILLING ORPHANS AND HIDING EVIDENCE THIS WAY.
72. C] EMBEZZLED. The Missing Person Reward Scheme Is A Big Scam. In Fact, A Police Reward $1million Secret $90000-Per-Account Round Syndicate.
Killing and Stealing Orphans' Houses & Creaming the Community.
73. D] CRIMESTOPPERS' ROLE IN ABETTING AND AIDING THE POLICE IN THE KILLINGS OF ORPHANS, STEALING OF THEIR HOUSES AND IN THE SHELVING OF CASES IS UNLAWFUL.
74. E] <u>The Perfect Orphans Laws And Their Rights To Their Own Property.: Extracts From The Book Of Creation</u>

F] Credible Evidence to Exonerate Alec Baldwin

I [David Gomadza] rest my case.

www.twofuture.world

I Represent YAHWEH On Earth.

Court of Creation on Earth

I summed up our finding about the whole saga in the book credible evidence to exonerate Alec Baldwin where I argued that all this killing of orphans and stealing their properties is

1. Abuse of Power
2. Harassment & Invasion OF Privacy
3. Illegal Collection of Capital Gains Tax Before Sale of Property
4. Targeting & Killings of Orphans

5. Illegal Spying Using Button Cameras

6. Killing the American Dream

7. Falsifying and Withholding Evidence.
Abuse of power

ABOUT THE AUTHOR

David Gomadza visit www.twofuture.world

WHAT CAN HUMANS BE AS PER THE BOOK OF CREATION

www.ingramcontent.com/pod-product-compliance
Lightning Source LLC
Chambersburg PA
CBHW031514210526
45464CB00007B/2911